Jack Ma: A Biography of the Alibaba Billionaire

D1795541

Entrepreneurs do not need to be inventors. An inventor who also has the skills to be a successful entrepreneur is talented indeed. It is vision that helps an entrepreneur stand out initially. The skill is to see an opportunity and seize it. In today's world, there are many entrepreneurs who have created enormous wealth to the extent that everything they touch seems to turn to gold. It is almost impossible to envisage them failing at anything, yet most have needed great resilience and in all likelihood, have suffered rejections and failures along their path to success. That is certainly the case with Jack Ma, the founder and Executive Chairman of Alibaba Group, and is estimated to be personally worth almost $40 billion.

Jack Ma is the name that the West recognize; he was born Ma Yun in Hangzhou in 1964 during Mao Tse Tung's Cultural Revolution. It was a time when China was isolated and in desperate need of development. Few would have thought that half a century on, it would be a massive market and a major player in the world's economy. Ma was one of three children, having an older brother and a younger sister. His grandparents had supported the National Party, Mao's opponents so times were hard for the family. It was perhaps this that taught him the importance of resilience, and gave him the determination to ignore rejection and pursue his ideas? In any event, it is one of the many prominent traits in his make-up.

He was an inquisitive child who wanted to absorb everything around him and he was especially determined to learn English. He used to go to a nearby hotel as a youngster because he knew it was where foreigners stayed so there was a chance to learn and practice his English. His city, Hangzhou, had become popular with tourists after the then President of the USA, Richard Nixon, visited in 1972 and so even though China maintained a level of isolation from the West, determined tourists wanted to see the place for themselves. It is now one of the most popular tourist destinations in China.

As part of that process of learning, Ma became an unofficial guide for foreigners wanting to see the city. He got to know a great deal through these informal channels, developing pen pal relationships and learning about the world outside China's borders.

He was full of ideas; his father was to warn him later that some of his ideas may lead to his imprisonment, yet he continued, and look at where he is today. He has managed to avoid any problems with the authorities, even though some of his methods along the way have been somewhat unorthodox.

At one time, he was a teacher but later he co-founded the Alibaba Group which ranks as one of the biggest e-commerce companies in the world. In the last full trading year, finishing in March 2017, Alibaba posted 56% growth with revenue of $23 billion. Contrast that with the figures for 2010 that show a sum of below $1 billion, and it is easy to see the astonishing growth rate as the world came out of recession.

His current shareholding is just a little under 8% with his other business interests including Beijing Enlight Media and Huayi Brothers, another operation in the entertainment sector. So, how did his success come about?

Since becoming famous, he has been interviewed many times; everyone wants to know his story. By his own admission, he failed school exams five times, two in primary and three in middle school. He twice failed his college entrance exam but after entry, he graduated with a Bachelor of Arts/Science from Hangzhou Teacher's Institute in 1988. He then began to apply for jobs, meeting with almost complete failure; KFC did not want him, neither did the Police Force. He applied to Harvard several times without success but then many people who are not outstanding academically would suffer the same fate there.

He would be most welcome to attend nowadays to lecture budding entrepreneurs who are learning the theory without ever having put it into practise.

He has described how his development was based as much on an informal education as a formal one. He learned to question things and that is something he continues to do to this day. He seemed to have a natural flair for weighing up the pros and cons whenever he was confronted with a problem, or needed to find an answer. He admits to a number of mistakes but clearly, few have had any lasting effect on his businesses.

Ma sought something that he could build for his future; he was having little success in his applications for work that attracted him. He began to teach English at the university he had attended but he did not see that as his long-term future. After all, although Ma was not especially money-orientated, his salary at the University was just $12 a month. He set up a business as a translator and while doing that, he was introduced to the Internet in 1995 when he was paying his first visit to the USA and trying to recover a payment due to a Chinese company. As he looked through the information it revealed, he noted that there was no mention of Chinese beer! China with a billion people! He realized that there was an opportunity that the Internet provided in general and promoting China in the form of its small and medium sized companies seemed to open a number of possibilities. What he was unable to do during his time in the USA was to get any financial support for his ideas, so when he started up, he had minimal capital.

His first step was to open "ChinaPage" with friends to tell the world more about Chinese business and what it had to offer. There was an immediate response to his listing of Chinese businesses with emails coming from many parts of the world, seeking partnerships with the companies that were listed. Clearly there were people in different parts of the world who recognized an opportunity, unlike those he had approached for financial support in his very early days.

Remember that the Internet has created a global market with electronic mail offering instant communications. That was not something that everyone saw back in the 1990s. His frustration with Chinese bureaucracy meant that he could make little progress. He had set up a partnership with a government body that held a majority shareholding but it merely led to Ma's frustration because of red tape. As a result, he quit only to take a post with the Ministry of Foreign Trade and Economic Cooperation. He met many influential people during that time and they included the founder of Yahoo, Jerry Yang who was to invest $1 billion with Ma a few years later, taking at that time 40% of the business.

Alibaba

Ma still recognized the opportunity out there and so left his post in the Ministry to pursue his ambitions. Before the arrival of the 21st Century, he decided it was time to have another try at the Internet and founded Alibaba.

The name "Alibaba" came from a brainstorming session. Ma had known the collection of Arabic stories known as "One Thousand and One Nights" and specifically "Ali Baba and the Forty Thieves". Apparently when Ma asked someone if they knew the story, the response was "Open Sesame" which were the words that opened a door to a huge treasure trove in the story. As he asked more people whether they had heard of Ali

Baba, most said that they had. He was a man that was seen as kind and generous and wanted to help others. He decided that was the name for him.

One of the real success stories at that time, and still so today is eBay which was one of the first companies to penetrate the Chinese market, offering a platform that linked consumers wanting to buy and sell. It charged users through its platform EachNet for every transaction. Alibaba was still looking at helping small and medium-sized businesses to go online and trade for themselves yet Ma saw that he had to combat eBay within China as an immediate task. He launched Taobao in 2003 in competition with eBay, and it charged no commission for an introductory period of 3 years. eBay's initial reaction was that it couldn't work because it did not have income, but Ma took the view that it could ultimately make money. He offered peripheral support to customers such as customized web pages for

a small charge. Gradually it grew at the expense of eBay and within five years eBay had given up the challenge and left the Chinese market despite its enormous size.

It had not been obvious to the outside world that Ma could succeed. He was rejected innumerable times by venture capitalists as he sought assistance. He must have been rejected 30 times before finally getting the support of SoftBank whose CEO, Mayayoshi Son, was another disciple of modern technology. It invested $20 million in Alibaba and Goldman Sachs provided another $5 million. Incidentally, Mayayoshi Son is Japanese, of Korean descent, and has established himself as one of the richest men in Japan, but even he could not prevent the dotcom crash when it came. It was a further setback for Ma who was faced with making a number of difficult decisions, cutting back, and economizing to save the business. He realized that he had tried to expand too soon, but hindsight is a wonderful thing. The experience of having to cut back and lay off staff was extremely unpleasant to

Ma. It was far away from teaching English and portraying a positive outlook for the future.

He decided to consolidate in China before expanding once again when the economic prospects looked better. The injection of money from Jerry Yang was a major boost and he was able to expand and saw his company, only six years old at the time, valued at $2.5 billion. Not that much more than a decade on, that figure is getting close to $500 billion.

Ma relinquished the post of CEO in 2013, but remained as executive chairman and he raised $20 billion on the New York Stock Exchange in an initial public offering in 2014, an astonishing sum for a company that was only 15 years old, and had lived through the dotcom problems and a worldwide recession.

Alibaba now operates in 4 commercial sectors; e Commerce, cloud computing, innovation initiatives, and digital media and entertainment. It holds an annual Singles Day each November and last year's figures showed a turnover of 3.8 trillion yuan (approximately $1 to 7 yuan), making it comfortably the biggest such event in the world. The mobile phone has transformed consumer behavior and will continue to do so, at the likely expenses of retail high street stores.

He has yet to make a profit in cloud computing but is seemingly unconcerned, and rightly so given the overall success of the Alibaba Group.

Not surprisingly, Jack Ma's success has been recognized by his being awarded several things along the way:

- In 2004, fairly early days, he was placed in the "Top Ten Business Leaders of the Year" by China Central Television.

- Just a year later, he was awarded 'Businessperson of the Year' by 'Business Week' magazine.

- Also in 2005, he was in the list of '25 Most Powerful Businesspeople in Asia'.

- In 2009, Ma was in 'Time' magazine's list of the 'World's 100 Most Influential People'.

- Also in 2009, he received the '2009 CCTV Economic Person of the Year: Business Leader of the Decade Award'.

- 'Forbes' magazine placed him as the 30th most powerful person in the world.

- He was 'Entrepreneur of the year' in 2015 at the Asian Awards.

Alipay

One of the real issues that eCommerce pioneers in general needed to address was consumer suspicion about providing their private financial information to buy online. They were uncertain about putting their personal card details into a laptop when they could not be certain that those details would be used for unauthorised purchases elsewhere. It was something that led the pioneers in e Commerce to accept that they may not be profitable in the early days and indeed, many were not profitable.

There is still some concern about hacking but secure payment gateways have largely overcome everyone's worries. Encryption technology and an effective "barrier" between the buyer and seller have eased consumer nerves. It was a real culture change for consumers to buy online, relying on pictures rather than being able to touch products in a retail store, and of course try them on when it came to clothing and footwear.

Ma's answer to the problem of financial security was to open Alipay, perhaps a name not as well known in some parts of the world as PayPal but every bit as powerful. He launched the platform in 2004 and today it has well over 500 million users. Purchases are settled with Alipay taking the money from an account holder and settling the debt in the appropriate currency. Obviously, the first stage is to register and provide valid ID information. A business must verify its legality and provide a prime contact. After successful registration, Alipay can be used as an alternative to credit or debit cards in making face-to-face store purchases. Alipay will want to see a legal document authorizing the stated person nominated as the point of contact has permission to fulfil that role before it will verify any application to register.

Alipay has established many partners over the years and is continually expanding its services to include restaurants, many types of stores, and even such things as taxi services and public transport. Now expanding as a global concern, it is usable in many countries and deals in several currencies.

It is now well-established as a "bridge" between companies and individuals, providing a service that removes any worries about the security of the Internet. It provides 90-day payment protection as well as full reimbursement for unauthorized transactions.

Jack Mapersonally owns 50% of Alipay these days. It is a vehicle that will always be successful as Internet trading is increasing year on year and secure payments are critical in that growth.

Tmall

Tmall began life as TaoBao and is now China's No 1 online shopping site; business to consumer. It has opened up the Chinese consumer market to traders from all over the world. It has rightly earned a reputation for quality, both in the service it provides but also in the products it sells.

In order to be registered with Tmall, a business needs to have a physical presence in China, though properly authorized overseas businesses can join Tmall Global. The obvious advantage of membership is the size of the Chinese market. Members have full control of the design of their presence so it is little different from having a stand-alone website. What is does offer is the size of the market that is immediately accessible to a company with good product to sell.

AliExpress

AliExpress opened in 2010 and provides a vehicle for companies to sell their products worldwide. It has become a place where consumers can buy almost anything so that it is not necessary to do anything other than check in, buy, and check out with all your shopping done.

As the name suggests, it is intent on providing an efficient and speedy service to anywhere in the world. Online shopping has become the norm in today's world and AliExpress's market share suggests that it has become a major player in that sector.

There is no fee for membership, buyers or sellers, and it oversees transactions, even down to a single small item and shipping is often free, and certainly quick. AliExpress operates an escrow policy which protects both buyer and seller because the money is only released once the goods have been received and the buyer confirms he or she is happy. It would be wrong to say there are never any problems because it is an impossible task to police every member completely because there are unscrupulous people that can provide answers to get membership approved without the intention of then acting honestly. There is a feedback system that buyers can check to see what previous customers of a supplier have said about the experience they had. AliExpress will help anyone making a legitimate complaint.

The "Shipping and Packing" section provides the details that buyers need to understand the process once they have made their purchases. There are express and standard postal services though on some purchases, it may not be possible to use a particular carrier or method of delivery. In any event, the buyer is provided with the precise options before purchase.

All the popular payment methods are available to consumers, including credit and debit cards, PayPal, and bank transfer.

Ma and the Chinese Entertainment Industry

Ma diversified very quickly into other business sectors and entertainment was one of them. Just as eBay had sought to take advantage of the huge market of China, as the country grew richer, an increasing number of ordinary Chinese people would have disposable income for leisure activities. A recent report that covers the years until the end of this decade predicts growth throughout the whole sector. It envisages a compound growth rate of almost 9% annually, twice the global average. It suggests that Ma's foresight in getting involved in media and entertainment years ago has been repaid.

- **Beijing Enlight Media**

This publicly traded company produces tv and films and its subsidiary Beijing Enlight Pictures Co. Ltd., is the third largest film distributor in China, responsible for 7.75% of the market.

- **Huayi Brothers**

Another player in the entertainment sector. Huayi Brothers is involved in film and television and has expanded into the Internet, licensing and music.

Huayi Brothers invested in Feng Xiaogang whose film about New Year was a great success and has broadened its scope into TV drama, artist management, records and entertainment marketing.

The future

Jack Ma is not someone to stand still. He has many years of a working life left and with his energy and determination, it is likely that he will succeed in his vision for the coming years.

He expects Alibaba to expand wherever new technologies takes it. He understands that things are ever evolving and while he may not think of everything, he is ready to embrace anything new that attracts him, or is proving to be a success.

His own view is that the whole job market will change; machines and artificial intelligence are both likely to result in the jobs market shrinking. The advantage of this "progress" is that it should improve the quality of everyone's lives. Ma is certainly willing to invest in this and recently quoted a figure of $15 billion set aside for that over the next three years.

He hopes to continue to increase trade across the globe and he still feels there is plenty of scope to help small and medium enterprises (SMEs) which was where it all began in the 1990s.

Last year, Alibaba announced an investment in Hollywood, Steven Spielberg to be precise. His company Amblin Partners are producing and distributing films in China and worldwide with Ma announcing a further $7 billion investment over the next couple of years. Spielberg's name in the entertainment industry suggests that this will be yet another successful collaboration.

Collaboration is important to Ma. Take for example the initiative to launch an electronic trade platform in Malaysia in partnership with the Government with the aim of creating more trade between the small and medium size companies in the two countries. His early experience with officialdom has not put him off working with government though he knows that it can be unwise to commit himself too much and find obstacles in his way.

It is part of an overall strategy to become even stronger outside the borders of China and South East Asia is an obvious place to start. The $1 billion that Alibaba invested in Singapore's Lazada has produced good growth there as well.

Famous Quotes of Jack Ma.

It is inevitable that someone who has become such a prominent figure in today's business world gets a great deal of media exposure. Such is his success that many people listen and many hope to learn. There are many quotes on different subjects and some reflect how he has moved from just an ordinary Chinese man to a world figure.

"We will make it because we are young and we never ever give up!" This was a reference to his struggle with eBay which was by no means certain to succeed. He was after all offering commission free deals for three years so it was natural that eBay was confident that it would prevail. This quote shows the real strengths of Jack Ma which are his drive and determination.

"Put the customers first, the employees second, and the shareholders third." Ma values the customers and of course began his adventure by identifying that small and medium sized businesses need help to reach the market that the Internet was able to provide them. They needed help, and still do, with Ma determined to continue in the future to open up the world markets for anyone who wants them. He is clearly less concerned about shareholders but anyone who has invested in Jack Ma is unlikely to regret that they did.

"If Alibaba doesn't get bigger and more successful than Walmart or Microsoft, I will regret it for the rest of my life. Our predecessors invested in us, it is therefore our (this generation's) responsibility to do better than them." Ma sees that it is natural to expect progress from successive generations. He is a living example of someone who has been able to grow a business from very small beginnings and certainly has plans for the years to come to expand even further.

"If the company always thinks of picking money out from the government's pocket, that company is rubbish! It should think about how to make money from customers and the market, and to help customers succeed." This is Ma's observation that companies should not be forever seeking subsidies; they should look for their own ways to develop their businesses through their own initiatives.

"The business schools teach a lot of skills about how to make money and how to run a business. But I want to tell people that if you want to run a business, you have to run the value first, to serve the others, to help the others – that's the key." While Ma is certainly not against academics as such, and may even go back to teaching one day, he is critical of the style of some teaching.

When he was called crazy in a Time Magazine article early this century, he was not offended at all. "I think crazy is good! We are crazy but not stupid! If everyone agrees with me and if everybody believes in our idea is good – we will have no chance."

"If you don't do it, nothing is possible. If you do it, at least, you have the hope that there's a chance." This seems obvious. Certainly, in Ma's case, he was happy to take a risk and clearly, he has been able to reach a point whereby even his setbacks have become insignificant.

"I use Thai Chi philosophy in business: Calm down, there's always a way out and keep yourself balanced, and meanwhile, don't try to kill your competitors." Thai Chi plays quite an influence on Ma, both in his business and his personal life.

"In this world, if you want to win in the 21st century, you have to be making sure that making other people become powerful, empower others; making sure the other people are better than you are, then you will be successful." Ma does not fear a situation where others become more powerful, even, it seems, competitors, because he has confidence in himself.

"I find that when a person makes a mistake or fails, if he or she always complains or blames others, that person will never come back from the failure. But if the person checks inside, this person has hope." Ma is happy to take full responsibility for his actions.

"My relationship with the government is: Be in love with the governments, but do not marry them." You recall in his early days, he was frustrated that bureaucracy hindered the progress of "ChinaPage." His answer is not to openly oppose a government but also not to allow himself to be hindered by it. Fairly recently, the Chinese government asked him to help solve a regular problem it faced with its ticket vending system crashing during the spring festival. He got his team to do it for free on the basis that the government would leave him alone.

"If eBay are the sharks in the ocean – We (Alibaba) are the crocodiles in the Yangtze River. Never fight in the ocean, let's fight in the Yangtze River." This is a great way to explain the approach he took in the early 2000s when seeking to develop his business in China, thereby preventing eBay gaining a stronger foothold than it already had. This ultimately

withdrawing from China, a huge m₹

"Today, people write about the successful stories of Alibaba. And I really don't think we were so smart, we made so many mistakes and we were so stupid at times. So, someday, the book I personally really will want to write about is Alibaba's 1001 mistakes. These are the things people should remember and people should learn." There is not a hint of arrogance in Jack Ma.

"Going anywhere, doing business, takes time. No market welcomes gamblers – You go there, create value for local people, have time – it will have chance." This was his observation when e said that it was difficult to do business in China.

"Never give up! Today is hard, tomorrow will be worse, but the day after tomorrow will be sunshine. If you give up tomorrow, you will never see the sunshine." This pretty much sums up Ma.

The World of Entrepreneurs

Ma's inquisitive nature and determination to solve problems stands out. In the early days of Alibaba, he understood that one of the obstacles he faced was consumers' fear about effectively sending money to China, as well as their general apprehension about providing personal details that may not be secure. In terms of the latter, it was the industry as a whole that gradually solved that but in the case of the former, he arranged to have Alipay launched without the permission of the Chinese banking authorities, a risk in itself to his personal freedom. Alipay is now bigger in global terms than PayPal.

He stands out from many of the top names today; he did not drop out of formal education like Steve Jobs, Bill Gates and Mark Zuckerberg. He graduated with an MBA from Cheung Kong University during the time he was building Alibaba. He is an academic himself, though he struggled with exams in his early days; he actually talks about teaching again in the future. The point was that he did not struggle with things he enjoyed and was passionate about; learning English is the best example of this.

Every entrepreneur understands that success is not automatic. In Jack's case, he certainly had setbacks along the way, but in some ways, he used them as motivation to keep going. He certainly was prepared to lead the way but clearly understands the need for teamwork, and has the character, even charisma and certainly confidence, to get people to follow him. A little patience is involved.

Every entrepreneur needs an open mind; ideas are great but there is the practical implementation to consider. It is important to be prepared to learn along the way, and embrace ideas which may be useful in pursuing any project. He can hire the best people to ensure that Alibaba is at the forefront of technology and not vulnerable to the developments within his competitors.

The Man

Ma remains a modest man, with fairly modest hobbies; he enjoys simple things like reading, poker, tai chi, and meditation. He did allow himself one luxury when he bought a jet plane for Alibaba which is always available for him when he wants or needs to travel, but otherwise there is little outward sign of his enormous wealth.

He became interested in the environment when someone in his wife's family became ill with the suspicion that it had been caused by pollution. He is now on the board of the global body Nature Conservancy, and spoke at the Clinton Global Initiative. There is now a new 27,000-acre nature reserve thanks to Ma's efforts. It would be great to think that he would one day put his name to several other environmental issues facing the world, and certainly the many endangered species around the world who are vulnerable because of their perceived value for traditional Asian medicine.

While he is often asked to speak, and regularly does so, he is also a very private person. He married a girl he met at school, Zhang Ying who openly said that she married him for his abilities rather than his looks. They have a son and a daughter, the son being an undergraduate at UC Berkeley in the USA.

There is little sign that he will slow down any time soon. After all, he has a vision of the future and while he has not reached his mid-50s yet, he is still relatively young in business leader terms.

Printed in Great Britain
by Amazon